Survival, evasion, & escape

for Mary,
& for the future,
let it be well —
Hank Malone
5/87

Poems by Hank Malone

EDITED BY KATHLEEN IDDINGS
La Jolla Poets' Press
P.O. Box 8638
La Jolla, CA 92038

ISBN: 0-931721-00-8
Library of Congress Catalog Number: 84-82407

Book design and production:
Mardel Findley,
The Art Room, San Diego, CA 92103

Printed in USA

To Alex, my son.

Contents

Acknowledgements—

Several poems in this book have appeared in print previously, in the following magazines: *Samisdat, New Lantern Club Review, Earthwise, Choice, Planet Detroit, Ontario Review, Wayne Review, Kayak, New York Quarterly, Chelsea, Grimoire.*

The author is grateful to the National Foundation on the Arts for their several grants, given in a variety of forms during the last fifteen years.

"... for just as actors who wish to cover the blush that rises to their forehead, dress up for their roles, at the moment when I am about to enter the world's stage where up until now I had been a spectator, I advance masked, "Larvatus Prodeo".

—Descartes

Survival

Binoculars nibble at the distant horizon,
tasting the rinds of the shoreline.
The sky is mildly recorded, without visitors.
Nothing but survival contaminates the water.
Everyday the herds are let out on the beach.
Everything is free to make itself tired.

The arrival of a new age, something new,
and nothing seems to change.
Another church. More worshippers. More
mechanical gods climbing out of blueprints.
More novels arrive. More yachts and distractions.
The harbor is crowded with dull magic.

The monotonous arrival of dreams and triumph!
Endless, the same, again and again
horizons, the same. Another triumph!
Endless triumph. Our bottles adrift
and returning. Our words drifting without light.
O, we are crazed without another Voice.

Mail

Half the people in America
never get any mail; they hide, without numbers.
And the other half are addicted
to the envelopes, and the zips. It's the center of their day!

If you're a professor of lost literature
you'll receive tiny bills and perfect-bound books
and Mozart-club brochures, and perhaps the long awaited letter
from a publisher rejecting your latest manuscript.

If you're young and handsome and in love
there will be the daily blue and pink love letters
along with all the muscle-mail. The love letters
will be soft, scented blossoms. O joyous love letters!

And if you are old and retired and stay indoors,
your mail will be huge and useless, with a lifetime
of insurance advertisements following you, and fold-out
death pamphlets with large pictures of vitamins and caskets.

And if you are like me, some days will be silent.
No mail. An utter mystery! Other days
there will be ugly crazy little letters, mostly
from the ex-wife. And sometimes a breathless poem from a friend.

I wish the mail would go mad one day, truly crazy,
so the old man could receive a love letter, and the professor
of literature could get one of my ex-wife's notes,
and the young lover would receive no mail, only mystery in the rain.

Survivors

my love goes out
to those people
in thick strange clothes,
working alone,
like the poet bukowski,
or georgia o'keefe,
drinking wine on lost days
or wandering the great mesas.

for every tough fighter
who carries genius into old age
there are a million meek bastards
who crucify themselves at 35,
leaving a drizzle
of incomplete politics
for the next generation
to suck on & ponder
in half-songs of confusion.

give me an old wizard
who knows a marxist
from a vegetarian,
& still knows how to vomit
when gangs of 20 year old poets
come to visit with six-packs of beer
& sticks of dynamite,
murderously talking
about the irrelevance of beethoven
& the death of illusion.

The lost library of alexandria

The best days have been used, the greatest money,
the happiest weather and the strongest energies.
Now the sheets wind with paler thighs, tangled with the night.

Everything is like a recollection of better days.
The world clutches more desperately, more distraught,
like an army of grave-diggers rising daily to hasten their burial.

We walk the streets in a world where hope has gone mad,
where it struggles, drugged and angry, gripping a long knife;
a dark machine that cuts crowds into shreds of arms and legs.

It is like a wild epidemic, so sudden! Families explode
and each child takes his wonderlost TV into a non-wondrous Light.
The future moves with deadly politics; men are stillfrozen with crumbs.

And everything is called Holy by star-haired prophets. The mind weeps
for lack of decent dialogue. The heart grows dim with poor branches.
Now the sheets wind with paler thighs, tangled with the night.

Origins

Robert Lowell is listening to the shortwave,
a C.O. in prison,
overhearing the voices of war in Europe.

Walter Lowenfels has opened another bottle
of Agua de Tehuacán Peñafiel
in the apartment of Diego Rivera.

Allen Ginsberg has cut out a SEND NO MONEY coupon
for a free trial of Bronchial Asthma Formula
from the back page of a Wonder Woman comic book.

Garciá Lorca has arrived in Madrid,
having no clear idea why the civil guards
are detaining him.

Robert Frost had dialed the last digit
of his sister's phone number,
waiting to tell her of the death of his daughter.

Marianne Moore has written
". . . with a letter from Dr. Doris Cochran,
Curator of Reptiles and Amphibians, National Museum."

and Dylan Thomas has stumbled from his stool again
at the White House, cutting himself
on the glass edges of a broken beer pitcher.

Carlos Williams has left his old home,
stopping at a gas station in Paterson
before driving to the hospital. He delivers a girl!

Wallace Stevens has entered a trance
amidst a large pile of insurance brochures,
with his bow-tie unhooked, and his wife in the next room.

Kenneth Patchen has just lost the use of his legs
and a SAVE KEN PATCHEN SOCIETY has been formed
to finance the first delicate operation.

and Pasternak in the far-off Soviet has begun another poem,
he has seen a great icicle breaking-off
and plunging into the water.

Wisdom

things are not so bad
if you're not busy trying to immortalize
yourself. i know that much.
if you're just walking down the street
& not working yourself into a sweat
over some new grey hairs,
life manages to come across
sometimes with all the security of a leopard
going after a gazelle.
some days you can just whistle along
& enjoy the toothpaste ads
& the cigar smoke & the telephone ringing
& even the voices of people
who don't care if you're dead or alive.

very little love is not so bad
& not such a strange way to live.
often you can drive a long lifetime
without a good kiss or a happy weekend.
decent people do it all the time.

one might even consider it wisdom,
if you could overlook the faces
& the tongues licking the frost of dreams.

We go together

i fold myself
over you
like a plumed bird over flames

my nightborn juices
plunge and sing

our seaweed
that gently sways,
salt gates at your world

i am from the other side
and you are the woman, standing
i am the creature-mariner
with my hands, ready to touch you

so much, down your thighs
at last unsheltered
my hands moving to your ankles
my mouth moving to your breast

home, o thou beauty, o
bend nearer as we count
our thrusts of heaven, heaves of earth
that sing the parable of our unity

the bird of passion clamors,
we are on another landscape

in luminous water, water
at the most ancient star
drowning our bodies beyond breath
taking such bold pleasure
in the image of our creation

Speaking of the composer, Max Reger

"at the age of 43 he had a heart attack and died."

i read these words on the page
& they frighten me.
i cannot say
"sech is life, vich likewise is
the hend of all things."
i am not charles dickens.

this morning my mother entered the hospital
for the X-rays, the barium enemas.
last night she was white-country sick.
everyone is thinking CANCER
but no one is saying it out loud.

if i should keel over at 43
i doubt that very much of me,
spaded, turned-over in poems,
would hang in the world very long.
i'm a second-rate mahler, a naked romantic
& i probably don't love myself
& so my little angelic poems
go unloved as well,
half-created, half well-written,

since worshipping art, laboring like a slave
with heavy words, elaborate plans,
is a terrible storm-lantern to carry.
& since to think that not a single line
will seize the world, or console a human heart,
is to think of cancer, X-rays, enemas, & death at 43,

my desire to write an immortal poem is an obsession.
& killing 763 people on a rampage with a rifle
(because i couldn't write a single great poem)
would clearly immortalize me!
the guiness book of world records would call it
a death for every scribble that didn't work.

What i want my son to Know

i want him to know the difference
between a tree
& a giant brain
that wants to sell him
a six-piece formica dining room set.

i want him to know
my love for him is boundless,
& something nearly holy,
& that if i become an old beast
roaring with my social security checks,
that he had my best love
when i was young & tough
& honest.

i want my son to know that power
can be direct as thunder,
or as sinister as knowing
it is better to say nothing
when you can grunt a warning to a friend.

i want him to know that heaven
can happen in the sweetness
of an hour, alone,
& there is all the joy
in building a single star.

i want my son to know
human speech like a multi-colored bird
bathing in the pools of morning.

i want him to know
that he is the noblest animal
to kiss the angel of pleasure.

i want him to know my chair.
my tree. my lady.
i want him to know his own chair.
his own tree. his own lady.

i want my son to know
how goddamned sick you can get
picking at the world's ass
to raise a dollar decently.

i want my son to know,
even if you're groucho marx,
that worms complete the cure
for everything
after the grey hair,
the losses, & the dying.

i want him to know
i was a goofy-guy like him
who sang with a staggering common voice,
i want him to know a common voice
& a temperate zone.

i want him to know that
a father & a son
are no bigger than two beans,
& that two beans
can know all the love in the world
because love is such a sightless word
with such a big smile on its face
that there is enough room
for all of us, no matter
how many mistakes.

this is what i want him to know.
that it's tough & beautiful
& that most of us will end up blindfolded
if we don't take the time
to taste the sweetness
as it passes from life to life.

Mortality

"BRR-AA-AA-AAATTTTTTTTTT!"
the sound of the old guy's stinking farts
knock around the brittle hospital ward.
he hides nothing from his wife anymore,
or anyone else, especially during visiting hours.
"B-ELLLLL-LLLLLCCCHH! BUU-UURRRR-RRP!"
he's only about 46
but cancer has chisled him down to an angry child,
layer by layer, artichoke-style
until now he's just a pile of selfish
farting bones
blabbing endlessly to his chubby wife.

one day you're walking around OK,
thinking you're immortal & wiggling your butt,
& then you step into a hole or slip on something
& the next thing you know
you've been half-swallowed away by some hospital
& you're facing a delicate operation
& some priest has just approached you about absolution
& 30 nurses are constantly taking little bits of blood
& pressure from all over your body,
& if you're lucky, really lucky, you'll survive
& walk out, swinging your suitcase, immortal again!

& maybe you'll even forget about that old guy & his farts

The fashion model

the fashion model
sprawls in her vocation
upon a great bed
of human homes.
her tiny breasts
enter the windows
like sunlight,
her pearl necklace
falls enormously
upon the green lawns,
her white arms
dip into the cereal bowls,
and her tiny polar-
blue feet go kicking
into the bookcases,
rupturing the bindings.
the earrings ignite
a thousand automobiles.
the roar is tremendous,
deafened by cologne!

the fashion model posing
hovers like a dragon
above the pit
of ivory bathrooms.
the washing machines,
moving with pitch-colored water,
receive the nervous
fragments of wool,
the cotton hands,
the invincible brassieres,
the forest of garments
from the tavern-smelling hamper.
under the fashion model
everything is transformed
into tangerine
feathers of intense delicacy.

the sun is obscured
by morning oils,
by lips, beautiful red

perfectable lips,
great clouds of lips
and oils, fashionable lips
opening and closing
like balloons, puffing and pouting,
growing pastel, exhaling red,
boundless rippling lips
and tongues losing themselves
in the diamond-shimmering of saliva
as the transparent fashion model
hoists one of her phantom legs
into the blue morning air
and the ring-finger of every wife
begins throbbing
on her clay-colored hand,
her tiny eyelids fluttering
in awesome servility
as the fashion model
turns devotionally
upon her bed
above the brick houses
unfastens her highway
of dark imaginary hair
and a thousand husbands at a time
drive up into the sky.

With this new poem comes fame and my picture on the covers of magazines

And certain women will run up
and treat me like a movie star.

Suddenly, i'll become handsome
and witty and perfect,

and other men will hate my power.
I'll become a famous victim of jealousy.

And soon a fragrant light
will hover around my head,

and women will whisper about it.
A great lover, the poet has become a saint!

Later, the universe will change course.
Slowly, it will approach me, and revolve.

It was inevitable
that i should die like this,

famous grey hair,
powerful baggy pants.

Antarctic diary

During a change of mood
the wind has brought back the snow.
I stand alone with my diary, chipping
the pages like porcelain as I write.
There is no mood like this changing
sky backing up like a field of locusts.
We are all without food.
Having never known such distress
we are utterly without hope.
The plunging temperature
will kill us all before dawn.
I have said my last prayers.
The last of the sled is burning
like a closing eye, close to death.
We are all wondering
what will happen when this black mouth
swallows us.
Blackboro thinks we will sink
into the half-crazed visions of Blake.
I am brutishly hoping for darkness.
The dogs have all changed
positions. Kings
lie with their mothers in the snow.

The girls at corporate headquarters

All in corporate-colored suits, the girls
emerged from their meeting, glowing like nuns.
It was all like what the men did, a Big Plan:
to write the complete history of their Leviathan
as it grew through the years, as it profited,
as shares split, as employees became laboring thousands
puzzling over strange tasks and low pay.

The girls left the corporate office at lunch-break
to seek out the grass beyond the asphalt parking-lot,
to skip and sit and to gaze, to hold squirmy little flowers
wagging in their hands, talking about The Big Plan,
to create a corporate history for every employee, even the janitors,
a book to explain the humble beginnings of Empire, and more, to wake
the soul of each limping worker with the legend of this Pyramid.

Chicken or egg

if i am a multi-national corporation
& know each time there's a divorce
someone goes out to buy furniture, cutlery,
& another mattress,

i may find a secret blessing
in all the bursting families & despair.
& if i am a child-psychologist or marriage counselor
i will be rich, & very concerned about divorce,

& if i am a married man with a wife,
some kids, surrounded by the sirens of liberation,
deteriorating income,
& death as my inevitable enemy,

o, i will smell the fragrance of
divorce & behave like a madman.

Few write antarctic

1.
American poets by the batch
send themselves to Europe
every few years
like a school assignment,
to verify Italy, France,
the pix in the text, to see
the difference between heroic
and colossal and drunk
and always to see
if their originality
will rise, like a hot Sienna sun,
to the occasion.

And the poems arrive, bowel movements,
a reaction of psyche to the pull-chain
water closets, the ubiquitous monarchies;
the wine, the endless churches, and ruins
gorged down with red peppers and medieval poverty.

2.
The Europe Poem is a letter home to America,
a wizened, "gee, mom, if only you could see . . .",
full of sensitivity, reactions to every reaction
produced by every reacting glance
to every lance and stone and inch of history.

There is usually a poem about David in Florence,
or Mont Blanc and Provence, the Plaza San Marco,
the Greek islands, even Madame Tussaud's.
In these poems, America is never flattered.
Hamburgers and the suburbs reach their lowest ebb
and home is despised, at least for several weeks,
until the homesick poems start faintly flowing;
humorous, ironic, really quite serious . . .
homesick for Kentucky chicken and a 'real' Coke.
A holy vision collapses into momma's arms.

3.
I say the poets should go to Antarctica
and forget Europe, at least till 50.

At 30 in 40 below
there would be no romantic horseshit
flung back to the American quarterlies
from a diarrhea of European poems.
Instead, the poems would be carved,
chipped away slowly on frozen paper
and every icy realization of this nadir world
would come along with lots of puffing suffering
and there would be no more cheap shots about liquor
and cold lovers.

The importance of everything would be known
or would remain dead silent, frozen in the poet.
There would be no 'Madonna of the Rosegarden'
at the South Pole, no buttons to push,
no easy allusions.
The snow and the sky would take on the whiteness of paper
and whatever was not white would be the heart.

self esteem

clumsy! not like the fish,
(how natural they seem) like party-guests
always so correctly dressed,
never a scale more or less;

i drop my silverware, underwear, anywhere.
clumsy i am with all this protocol;
i don't recall the names right, or books.
damn! shall i dress, or wear no clothes at all?

ignored by everyone & everything,
my feet end up on the plates.
i wish i knew to leave my tongue at home,
or heart, or my gun, but which one? my fate

is so absurd, stumbling in delicate blades of grass,
& my body is such nonsense filled with poison.
i dream of a natural kind of life
& then my elbow slips into the soupy reason;

i am such a mistake, such an ass!
listen, it's tough to live alone inside
with three hearts, an ugly face, & a stinking groin.
"howya doin", you say, & i'm swept away by the tide.

Evasion

The man standing
with his arm on the bar
speaks a foreign language
understood by everyone:
sea water.
There is a great porpoise in his voice,
a great porpoise and a squid.
With moving gills his words
rise and disappear.
Pressure-changes torment him.
He puts on his hat with eight arms.
My vision is blurred! It is clear,
under the deep sea our life changes.

The King

his bleached lips are unraveling at 45.
they sink into phone calls to Chicago
or Kansas, begging money, half-way to ruin.
a phantom cathedral in middle age.

at 45 he leaks sludge from his clothing,
sits naked and obese, swaying in lard
in his downtown-throbbing hotel room,
humming black rhyming melodies through a gunsight
whine some sharp fox with her unzipped snout in the mud
dyes his hair dark curling leaves of slime,
washes her fingers, fitting his cold-blooded head
with a long-blossoming nylon stocking.

there's a little king
in all of us.

at 45 dumping money overboard,
showing up with his green dream-roll,
the five-foot mausoleum of a man
runs wildly from an offal whimpering in his blood,
every encampment wrecked by implaccable creditors,
every ring taken eventually from every hazlenut finger,
the muzzle is haunted by his mainspring.

monstrous at 45 in soup-green suits
with a wife detonating somewhere,
forgotten crash of the home not seen in months,
eight entire children turning into black diamonds
as the pudgy hotel-fingers enter the sea
and the clotting-acids devise a fragrance,
an echoing of eyelids, a deep carnal taste and swallow.

emerging each day
without teeth, raw gums, his miracle voice
chipped loose from the other side of the moon,
rambling the long drumskin route of his life.
professional spider and pimp, gamer and dodger,
huge bottles full of deranging lubricants
closing his eyes, reminiscing
in the death-beds of vacant flesh and ears.

how is a man living? the smell is plucked out.
he can't help himself.

there's a little king
in all of us.

one doorway-day he'll show up to the broken home
repairing in front of his dangling wife, explaining
in black pants and violet tie, massing his perfume,
a helpless loving letter of Introduction.

and next week dreaming luminous again,
the week after he'll begin a new industry,
be off 'in show biz' into the tenement viscera of another fox,
leaving his gone-to-bone-wife to the winter,
scrawl upon another bedroom his slaughtering thirst,
fall again almost-innocently into his wrinkled trail of fire.
the ocean is not his, why do they pursue him?
why do the freezing women follow him into the Ocean?

ugly and withering hedgehog,
transparent carnival-wonder of doomsday,
on his desperate shoulders
hang the city green-lights of cloth,
the kingdom of the fibre above the flesh.
upholstered about the disfigured fault of his presence
the clothing takes the sudden bright color of blood.

the suavity, the bulking of clothing,
the king, more insolent, widening, mouldering at 45,
pursuing every oxen-ecstasy that pursues him,
eating at the consuming bark of eternity
he learns in the deathless shine of shoe-leather
there is a pavement that pities bedlam.

there's a little king
in all of us.

and what do the foxes see in the icy bald hemisphere?
what pleasures run from his mouth
into the glacial moons of flesh beside him in the dark?

where are they climbing on this deathly buddha?
life is flickering here at the end of the human road.
and each new child haunts him with the same solitude
in each final pendulum-flame of the candle.

who am i? what life have i just lived?
who are the moons loving me in this loud derelect?
45, deep in terror under each grey hair,
nobody knows. laughter, and everything is dumped into her ditch.

Sam Spade, therapist

She walked into my office like a single mauve glove,
ready to pay, pay hard with her heart
for my ear, for my reflex, for that white carnation
of support in my attentive eyes.

Blonde, slim, and forty-six; a sex-crazer once,
skin tight now, with too much sun-lit tennis,
too much bikini-tan, expensive booze.
She overflows, she pours me a bourbon-glass full of years.

Legs crossed well, she sat like a knicknack, in a woman's first
wintercold twilight, touching her own mortality;
her body, her blue eyes, her breasts, they could
just no longer dependably shove around her men.

Where that deep bank-account of other's lusts had been,
in the curve of leg, and throat - now
there was only tough cash, that green and familiar mold
that grew deep around a golden aging gravel-throated soul.

Money and lawyers and talk of divorce,
hours of property-talk, and the grief-talk about the kids.
The best I could do was to mop up her tears,
help to harden the heart, prepare for the ice-age,

create plans that were sane and hellish and aggressive,
like stashing the jewelry in deposit boxes and changing the accounts.
What a pot-boiler, and what a journey! To help steel the heart
of such a fading beauty; to sit there

in those tough sad flurries, only to help sock out the lights.

Publishing poems

somewhere in this world
someone is reading one of my poems.
later, he'll probably pick
his nose to death
& then call up his girlfriend.
"hello, phyliss?"
maybe they'll go out for fish & chips
or gumbo or vichysoisse
or weiner schnitzel.
"listen," he'll say,
"i just read this terrific poem."
& she'll be sleepy in his arms,
too tired to listen.
later, one of them will burp
into the darkness.
we are not fools.
poetry is a fragile bridge to be crossed.

The menagerie

THE FISH: i am a fish, with stupid headlight eyes,
nowhere to go but through time, circling around,
circling over nothing, rising toward nothing, and
merely shining back when others speak to me.

THE APE: i am an ape, bending over my banana,
picking into my ears with my feet, howling
with the other apes, masturbating to pass the time,
picking my nose carefully in front of an audience.

THE BEAR: i am a bear, plunging through the swamps
on my spongy feet, sleepy in enormous hunger,
drowsy in my brutal attacks, like a silly giant
i cheerfully take what i want with my teeth.

THE LAMB: i am a lamb, bleating my sadness
to everyone, losing myself in order to cry out;
my hogging little body, fat with innocence,
always just slow enough to be caught and killed.

THE BIRD: i am a bird, always preening my wings:
flight has become so dull, always rising above everything.
i wonder if there is another kind of flight, beyond this,
or whether i should learn, again, how to live on the ground.

THE LION: i am a lion. my wife spends the money,
brings home the meat, raises the children,
and when she nudges me in bed, i roar so loud
that i am crowned and feared by everyone.

THE ELEPHANT: i am an elephant, without recollection,
with skin too thick for worldly penetration.
tragedy is something i must invent within myself,
within this safe, thick skin.

THE SNAKE: i am a snake, with mystery in my movement,
sliding across, causing a danger to everyone.
people would like to kill me. i am so depressing.
but there is a mystery i cultivate, in my sliding, keeps me alive.

THE POET: i am a poet, inside me fighting

with all the other animals, taming each quality, rending, subduing each skill, each chill, haunting the deeps, a creature searching for a creature never seen before in the menagerie.

The women of Andromeda

rape scene. working all day in america,
stopping at the cleaners for my pants.
enters the most beautiful woman in the world,
she's uncanny, and i want to cast my world
in her flesh, her smile, those overtaking eyes.
everything's like a signal yearning for this body.
o it is all i can do to ignore her legs!

women entering rooms, into a man's plumbing
straight-away, compelling love with their movements
pouring out of a sleek and sliding grass,
wild muscles perfect in a body of gold,
straining thighs, a tremor of free-falling curves.
o the simple body entering life like a menace,
every place the same, these women who open my wounds.

Ambition

The panthers of our life, the million dollar people,
the politicians, the ambitious ones; the men
and women bellowing cross-eyed and blue-suited,
victorious at public crowds in great arenas,

have you noticed how often the ambitious people
are from Ohio, or New Jersey, or Nebraska?
Or grew up in ghastly poverty, on muddy streets, confused
and whipped around by their faded, stalk-chewing families?

A monster in some old hungry pit of the soul
is usually lurking at the source of any decent ambition,
and if you introduce me to some swell empire-builder
I'll show you scars more crude and sad than a drug-addict's veins.

Ambitious people, they're the opposite of drowsy farmhouses;
ambitions are crazy with dancing and dangerous obsessions all night.
And I really love ambitious people, the tough strident kids,
but usually it's what's hidden I like best: the complexity, the argument.

I nod with all the sad and wild things that surface in the end,
in biographies: "She was raped five times by her brother and then
watched her mother stabbed and her father shot, and. . ."
All the hot needles of our sperm and nurture finally make some sense.

O, when I meet a panther on the washed-out, push-cart streets
(and I've met a hundred in my own mirror) I want to yell out:
"Go fuck your sharp old teeth!. . . I want to ride you, Storm,
just to ride you, just to feel the rhythm of our high old Hell."

Notes and omens

Today we were apart, out of range,
this improvement over yesterday's wreckage.
Things better now with me drunk and delicate,
long wife in a novel late at night.
No change in our lovemaking, a good bed.
A tourist, a thousand beds, quite depressing.

The argument runs: nothing so essential,
see a bullfight, the Colosseum, a church. Thousands!
Here is your strange chance in history.
We walk fifteen miles a day on melting streets,
and we sense the failure of too many prayers.
Here's an eroded cannon carved with lions and saints!

I am sick of this posthumous tenderness.
My ideals are with my people, rinsing things out!
What kind of love is for a Roman ruin?
You become a scholar working in those grains of dirt,
you develop a taste for sand and for stone ears.
Soon you begin expecting to hear from God.

The phone-call-to-E.E.-produced-nothing poem

Puffing on the old meerschaum
late in the afternoon
a perfectly ordinary day
where the rope of sex
just hangs in mid-air,
i think of the phone call
10 minutes ago, that went nowhere.

It was like walking into a drugstore
and buying a pack of gum
and walking out again.
The phone call was supposed to
go somewhere,
perhaps flattery,
perhaps a scratch behind the ear,

some new and cynical gossip,
some ghostly talk
or suggestion of sex,
perhaps a laugh or two.
But there was no luck.
Here was a phone call
that just didn't work.

It was a call between
2 shop-keepers,
a call full of frosted gestures
and the gentle daily boiling
of the planet,
a phone call they will never squeeze
into a book of delights.

America, early 1980's

It is the fashion
to be financially secure,
especially when everyone else
is dismally poor.

This leaves 43 states pretty empty,
the midwest gone, there's only cows and moos.
And California's become
the fat of a heap, full of Hollywood and booze.

Michigan, Nebraska
are worse than shit:
Michigan men have big necks, bad feet
and Nebraska fingers do little but knit.

Our magazines explode with new truth and youth:
CALIFORNIAN'S HAVE ALL BEEN CURED OF SOMETHING!
And on the prairie all have gutter-jobs and disease.
In Ohio, Lord, it's all rubber-heads and nothing.

So if you want real fashion and security
then move in with town-and-country blondes,
and for good prospects, marry those poets of California,
all of them: ink, and ocean-minds, and bronze.

Bukowski at the moon shot

The poets were all there for the moonshot
along with old, rusty, booze-nosed journalists
and the politicians, an avalanche of chromed-up bodies.

The poets were all drunk, as usual, staring into
the blinking steadiness of the stars tinkling above them.
And the poet bukowski was there, his doomed face ready for comedy,

drunker than most, nightmaring at the edges.
When the rocket left the firing pad and the journalists scribbled,
bukowski turned to the flanking generals and said:

"history has chance after chance to prove men fools,"
and then he turned his booze bottle up like a coronet, a little rocket,
and trumpeted songs and simple fables to wash down the launch.

He pointed up at the rocket that was tilting off like a cut flower
and said, "Beware bad food and excessive labor," shaking his head.
And he was right. The moon became our tragedy. Just an old
pincushioned map.

there is something to help you sleep

You are in bed, yet haunted and awake,
thinking of the deep-sea fishermen,
rising to the thought of Rome or Acapulco.
Nonsense! The airplanes wander the heavens

dark and drunk with tortured men.
You are better off in bed nervously dreaming
on a diet of handsome doubts,
trimming the fat off your crazy ambitions.

Imagine yourself in Cannes.
What would you do with your astonishment?
The cognac would embalm your wits.
You would find yourself all roots, without blossom.

Take it from one who has seen the world.
You are frightened of women and laughter,
and for the same reason. Only inches away,
regions as unexplored as Mars.

Barnstorming

Poets reading their brains out
from campus to campus
down through the girlish tears of America

and all we recall
is their painted
public-egg personalities.

Who thinks of a single poem
thinking
of our favorite new poets?

Bukowski drinks
down hallways of brutality,
and Kicknosway walks on four claws.

Berryman jumps
from the twin-city bridge,
and Plath dies in a noxious bell-jar of fury.

Ai is singing "ai, ai, ai,"
and wandering the Minnesota snow there's Robert Bly.
These poets all seem the offspring

of Harpo Marx,
and the poems come from poetry-honking horns
running back and forth across a student's stage.

The women poets are so sexy
they demand centerfolds,
and specially-made brassieres.

And a man who writes poetry
has got to make love to half the campus
or else he's nothing but a phony fart and a footnote.

I am waiting for a hunchback
reading aloud, with a purple eye,
to read a single line I'll recall forever.

It is true, I am weary of poets
who make me wonder
what they're like in bed.

Will I ever read again
a poet who receives wonderful messages
from sunflowers,

images and music that aim
to peel the skin off the planet?
That's what I want to hear.

I am so tired of poets and their madness
and their lumber jack brawling
and their watermelon tits, and rear-ends.

Let the poets dream awesomely
to cause a ferocious waking in my ear!
Let their books undress their show-business.

Is anything better than sex?

"When the editors of Psychology Today magazine asked their readers, "Is anything better than sex?", 75% of those Americans who responded said yes. Some 81% of women said sex was not the best thing in their lives. Among activities listed ahead of sex were: "accumulating money" and "eating Haagen-Dazs Ice Cream."

-Magazine section of the Detroit News, Feb. 26, 1984

O there is a hunger
and the hairy fist of a journey
but not toward the flame of sex . . .

the joy of roads sweeten
toward the snowroses of chocolate and ice cream,
and toward the plow-horses churning green dollars

up from the bloodless sub-divisions of real estate
where shoddy whisper-thin bricks hug and kiss
in a horrible circle of streets and driveways.

Speak of heaven's soft, wide-eyed instrument,
(with each heart aching for open aerial embrace)
and speak of deaf dollar-ears and icy-cream mouths

searching dumb for reasons to plunge love deeper,
fish-eyes preparing to stare, but not pricelessly embrace!

I come to you with wonder

As in God's hand
giving her to me,
i reach out
like a boy finding a star.

I shall love you
as pleasure walks in the shade,
as roses speak
upon the land.

Your voice
is the lover's moon,
and there is a delicate room
where the bells ring only for us.

Lie beside me now
and let all wisdom pass.
Let the hour of our silence come
to raise its magnificent head.

A kind of love, recollected

It was a shimmering voyage all the way,
it was a horse-ride, endless,
and now, long returned, we civilized beasts,
we've each forgotten us
our names, the details, the light touch
of whatever we whispered and saw in the night.

Now, here, what fills my eyes: the song,
and lingering in the song itself, the simple luxury:
we were strangers crumbling in passion,
complete in our frenzy of sheets and nakedness,
embracing, all arms, buttocks, tongues,
all passion, a hundred times, dearly.

And we came to know our gurgling speech, almost silently
in each other's sun-glazed flesh, no longer phantoms,
now in some wild abundance of fragrance and tears
and that holy praise that comes only in beds.
We made no final speeches, we were gone. Our bodies
had said everything with fullness.

The beautiful woman

I

Ask the poet, launched between her thighs,
ask him, Freud said, about beautiful women;
ask the poet who loved one, or thought he did,
and he'll tell you he was exalted by a thousand ships.

Beauty, beauty; a woman is killed off by her beauty;
all the sunlight it nourishes inside, colliding in the poet's
moonlight, a collision ignited! The outcome must be senseless.
The poets ring all the tragic notes in stories of beautiful women.

II

Beauty doesn't know its doom and beauty isn't nature's darling.
The gift corrupts a decent heart; foul sweat
but never happiness is the constant call of the beautiful woman,
and a man is mad who believes he can possess her!

A beautiful woman belongs to fiction, in the dream-soaked world
that lies in lightning and the poet's sperm in unrecorded fantasies.
Great passive beauty serves only to castrate. Rivals are everywhere.
A man in love with a beauty is surrounded by enemies

and like some ancient diety her power rises to become absolute.
Beauty which is all-loving may always resign itself away.
Show-piece from the start, she is the great total force
that leaves behind the most perfect maternal abandonment: desolation.

III

The poet may rise to the challenge and launch his battle with Incest,
yet, it is Menelaus who buys the final property; the piece of stone,
the beauty-turned-hostile, and cold contempt becomes the only match,
as the old fairy tale comes true to love, beauty is enslaved by the beast,

for Helen of Troy, who dreamed so much for herself,
launched impossible dreams in men,
and as beauty, alone, falsifies our true life
its legend is defiled by the poet, the man-turd, the breath, the beast!

I don't need anyone to help me suffer

Suffering is its own special game — solitaire,
    crippling boredom — nightmare
    obsolescence — lone empty volcano
    inconsolable heart.
I don't need anyone to help me suffer.

Lives of loneliness don't need anyone,
    but my life — i need everyone
    i need you — we must all help our dreams
    i am born into multitudes to love.
I need everyone to help me love.

Genetics

By the age of forty
it is clear,
we are each infected
with a million years of ancestry,
each of us, alone,
hovering under some wooly personality,
soaring when we can,
depressed when we can't;
the body's chemistry
in a multitude of innocent tributaries
commands our behavior —
our triumps, our daze, our griefs,
our loves, and looks, and all our top-heavy moods!
Our entire philosophy is the simple
residue of our chemicals, buttocks and brains,

our bodies annointed with carbons
and hydrogens. We cry out, speak,
and doodle in little notebooks,
all with less than the tiniest spark of control.
The best among us, among the species,
live and love widely, unbolting
impossible doors, taking all the honors
and feeling blessed, always blessed.
Clear, by the age of forty, our profiles
so clearly ancestral; we,
soulless kaleidoscopes
of energy and blind habit,
prologues to some newer prologue.

Morning somewhere in the city, featuring drunks, grass, sparrows, and schoolchildren

Starting with drunks at 7 a.m. it all unravels
Out from the raw quilt endless river of hours
Commensal with the short dew-sweating grass of the bone
The sparrows blaze with asphalt heat in the cafeteria
The drunks are moving furniture an ordinary automobile
Drifts into the picture like a huge condemning platitude
The schoolchildren owned like small Canadian villages
By the shareholders of all the similar corn-fed scholarships
Pull at the coats of the drunks small nests argue
With scraps of indifference tearing feathers from the halcyon
Abominations of the drunk's whisper glands and razorblades
Torn out of memory and hallucination sparrows building music
Like scripture in the large dormitories hidden from the world
Morning opens its mouth on the nearest fiend with a hammer

And the smash is heard like a guinea pig in scientific experiments
Handwriting goes up in the air a great illiterate X
Caught in the early sun a primitive web signs away everything
But life itself a feverish wine-colored life hanging
From a transom sleeping in the sun nothing saved
Absolutely nothing but the great lopsided sound of life
On a hot morning in the dead silence of a parking lot
It all unravels starting with the sinking of a ship
The stiffening of a snake the footfall of some monastic order
And the great drunks of the universe their mysterious seed
Each piece of helpless rag develops something blossoms
A pencil-sketch stumbling life-sized in free-falling clothes
Something writing in the sky attracting everyone's attention
Huge tailspinning figures spelling out the names of the great Beast

Snowstorm

Greendale avenue
reaches up, takes my footprint,
pulls it down
into the storm,
buries it in minutes.

I move, warm with liquor,
to the railroad crossing.
My ghost hovers
behind a non-inflammable
liquid-nitrogen truck.
The answer to everything is "75P3156"
on the tail of a Jones transport hauler.

Dear greybrains
broadcast
the spirit of the snow
on the radio.

In front of the auto store,
shoveling, shoveling,
looking for something,
stumbling, weak, disappearing.

God goes trudging
in this bleak weather.
Snowflakes like Oklahoma families.

A good stiff drink
muffles the earth
and opens the grave.
And there's that hell-breath
of the poor bastards
caught in the wheel.

Adaptation

I

looking
from a hundred miles above
the planet,
the civilization
made by men
and expensive wives
and crazy laws
and bad breath
and dead armies
. . . it's all invisible!

the planet
resembles
from a hundred miles
a fat bluejay
made into a snowball!

II

looking at
magnified 5000 times
a female mosquito
on my arm,
human flesh
becomes a haunted terrain,
a garbage-dump,
a cratered moon-scape,
a moon-forest!
the slaughterhouse
where the mosquito's
hypodermic nose
is buried
into the blood-well
below
is a jagged world
full of oily filaments
where the sun has gone
sickly blue.

III

now, looking
out the window
at what's familiar,
the cirrus clouds,
the dirty pigeons,
the empty wine bottles
half-hidden in the green shrubbery,
this morning
it is all a great consolation!

my consolation
lies in familiar perspectives,
familiar agonies.
i walk into a drugstore
and buy toothpaste
and God, i am right here,
right on the ground
and not too close
but not footloose or falling away!

an empty wine bottle on the grass
consoles.

Playing the wrong games

"nobody intends to play the wrong games"

- Anon.

And why am I not writing fine symphonies,
appearing arm-in-arm
with Hollywood beauties?

Why has the Oscar or the Pulitzer
or a million dollars
eluded me for so long?

How did I reach this middle age
so witless, talented, and disorganized,
so full of ideas that no one wants to hear?

Each question is a Chinese box,
and my best ideals fail me at every turn.
Now, all I can think of is fame, and being loved.

Somebody gave me the answer once:
"you lack the energy and the luck and the genes."
So, if the species point elsewhere, you end up a poet

or a clerk, biting your tongue,
fucking around with a thousand paperclips, erasers,
working the stub of a pencil until it shrieks.

what you don't expect to hear in a poem

In poems
you hardly expect
to hear
about
a crazy man in a madhouse
kissing the walls,

and you never really expect
to hear the poet
ask you
to send him
a five dollar bill
or a bag full of snails
or a dead rat.

And you never expect
the poet
to be caught peeking
through someone's window,
peeking
at some lady's leg
who's just stepping
out of the shower.

In most poems
the grass
is growing
pretty well
next to the riverbank
and no one is smoking it
or saying
"hey, this shit's some mixed jive!"

Yet poems
can ride bicycles
backwards, like this, and
poems can
sit on big fresh cream-puffs

and leave your pants
profoundly
soggy,

and poems can do practically
anything
except elect a president.

poems can walk up to Jesus Christ
hanging on the cross
and ask what's all the misery about?

And you can always stop
a poem
that goes round
and round in your head
by simply jumping off
a high romantic bridge.

Hot, straight and normal

From an obsidian age that brings you
little but the ominous crashing of windows,
nothing but cancer and bullet-holes and blood-stains,
I bring you one who runs hot, straight, and normal.

He doesn't care about progress or politics,
or unemployment, or God, or radioactive fish,
and he doesn't care about Wall Street or pelicans
or the beauties of twilight or the ethics of Kant.

Our young hero, who laughs and doesn't smoke,
is in perfect weight, exercises often, and works
with his eye to a computer, all day, in love
utterly with money-making programs and new soft-ware.

His only allies come with the silent paymasters
and a folly of men who bowl in winter and golf in summer.
He has a wife and two children he's never seen.
Never seen, never heard, never touched, never desired.

It seems a grand way to build a species;
create the man of perfect weight, prudent diet,
and the deep emptiness behind the eyes; the passive
born-again stranger who credits his way through the shopping malls.

Here is the man of the new American age; hot, straight,
and normal; never missing a beat, always drifing
as if he were marching, always moving slowly toward,
marching toward some ghostly stockyard, stockyard of men.

Zombie

Drugged, strange hat-topped people
Waddle down the street like ducks,
A cluster wearing frogskin and nadir
Silently following themselves to the van, after bowling.
Drugs keep them alive, no more than half-sane,
Tranquil and trembling in the juice of their ashes.

Words like "thought" and "pride" are meaningless
In this little cluster of Thorazine and Mellaril.
Words like "confusion" and "extinction" and "fatigue"
Are the only words that make any sense to anyone
And yet, for this little cluster, no words make much sense.
Like some hardbreathing amoeba moving along an iron coast
This troop moves zigzag, tumbling from meal to meal
Without substance, cut down; our silent shadow-family.

The rich

The rich don't need to hear anything you say.
The boredom of their faces, rising like patient steam,
is nothing but pure blindness to your soul.

What could you possibly say to an aristocrat
who has been so rich for thirty generations?
What words mustered as their huge yachts loom into dock?

You may scream like a choirboy that history will defeat them
but their perfect gaze, perfect grooming, will echo
they have always survived your silly dreams of history.

The rich have learned how to live, and how to die,
and they have arranged this very well. And you,
you have only made an art of being loud between the two.

The death of Marlon Brando, Orson Welles, and the Canadian Pacific Railroad

Of course good men
don't need heroes, or myths,
but we're not good men
so we need Brando on the waterfront
and Orson Welles behind the camera with his kane
and sometimes we even need Randolph Scott
and the entire Canadian Pacific Railroad!

I know, if we were all fine and holy souls
nobody would pay attention to gossip
and no one would think of Brando as fat
in Tahiti or Pago-Pago or ranting the obvious
with Indian Russell Means on the Today show.
If we were just good men enjoying life
it wouldn't be so sad to see Orson Welles
sucking away at cheap wine in TV commercials,

and it wouldn't be so sad to think of our astronauts
as political shits or recovering alcoholics
or grey-suited PR men for the airlines.
If we really felt so find about ourselves
and made love a lot and laughed and wrote good poems
then no one would feel crummy that Bogart was just a fantasy
and that Bukowski, our best poet, was taking the pledge
in order to hold onto another decade.

But we're just not good and decent men!
And so we stalk around like the undelivered Jim Dickey,
getting drunk, insulting women,
and madly daring to re-write the Bible, and Dashiell Hammett.
Hell, none of the poets I know is worth a damn.
Like snails we climb the walls, and then climb on each other,
and the poet's gossip becomes the pot-belly of our national crimes.

Movie night on television

I have no great expectations,
only the one on my television set, the film
with john mills as pip, alec guiness
his stout chum, the story
of a young working stiff (the kind who blacksmiths
on the moors and puts potatoes
whole in his mouth with a knife),
who suddenly falls down some coal-chute
into wealth and independence.
It seems all a kind of deus ex gothic
ex hollywood ex cathedra
david lean god-awful collossus!

Pip goes to a lot of giggling aimless parties,
learns to eat with a fork, and buys top hats.
He squeaks into the leisure-class
like blood-pudding passing for caviar,
until an awesomely dull woman (whom he has
"always loved") consents, godnose why,
to run off into this life with him.

I watch all these great expectations
of the working class
just go down to hell and bonkers,
stupidly walking themselves
into the grainy, celluloid twilight.

My own sex rope dangles aimlessly
as i turn off the television and wander around
in my humid home for half an hour,
once again resuming my search,
hitting the t.v. again, with great
expectations.

Now it is peter sellers, as inspector clouseau.
I feel better. He is a fool and a frog
and, like us, he will win in the end. More to my taste.

Light is our only messenger from the stars

I am sitting in my orange summer form.
It is hot, and somewhere there is gospel music.
There are radio telescopes!
I am restless trying to think of 3×10^5
in my undershirt. I feel like an animal,
not far from the jungle or the stars.
The world appears in all its silence.
Different layers of rocks and fossil. Brothers!
my heart speaks of the same radioactive rot.

The earth has not existed forever.
What a mistake! What an impressive moment!
Yet, we aren't rare, only 10^{10}.
There seems so little life in a universe,
I must try haunting this overwhelming heart.
Everything is so very finite.
We can explore only that part of things
which can send us its light.
Life lives at close-quarters with its questions.

When will this speculation reduce me to 20×10^9?
It is an artless universe I explore.
Chapters separate and recede.
There is a time ladder for my organic substance.
There is so much silence dragging us along.
There are a million inhabited planets
living in the flesh alone. And there are times
when I can hear the fate of another living world
change into rocks and metal.

Health food

The fact that Hitler was a vegetarian
and Jesus a drinker of wine
is barely an argument against
people who worship yogurt, and soybean hamburgers.

It's only the beginning, enough to provoke
bone-thin, purple wheat-eaters to say:
"But I feel so very good, so very healthy."
Yet a man who's drunk feels perfectly healthy!

And those who drink ginseng tea and mulch their sprouts
don't care that cocaine makes you feel like God.
Vegetables don't chew the arguments of blood-guzzlers;
each knows whose obituary will hit print first.

Children of Halloween

This little world
marches up and down hushed streets
shrieking and yelling
to every torch-lit porch.

These little primeval humans
scuffle along in cheap dresses
and rubber-plastic faces
screaming for candy and pennies.

And the sad grown shadows of adults
ascend from doorways with fingertips of chocolate.
"Here you are. . . and here you are." Like creamy pullets
this little world is caged by chicken-feed.

Five Haiku dawns

a dreaming of light,
darkness
prepares to sever its belly of stars

*

a long silver blade
honed
on the edge of the eastern horizon

*

a drawer is slowly opened,
the daylight
searches for its clothing

*

the stars are collected by the birds
and the eye
opens in the great commotion

*

the feathers of an owl
dust
morning-frost from the pond

For the little girls multiplying out loud

into eyes
where one can see
deserts, and beyond
where the future has been opened
and there is nothing but a dark canyon,
tears and blood for a river,
men entering and leaving hopelessly,
doors opening, eyes closing,
hearts without a future,
your little faces loving underneath.

into eyes
falling asleep in great crowds,
the well of tears is deep.
the lights in the womb
are cool cathedral candles.
life burning in a prisoner's sperm.
doors closing, and eyes entering
the lonely ashes of life,
litle faces never without hope,
loved by all sorts of ruin.

A death in Venice

How many little poems are written
in paris or venice sitting outside a cafe,
a small set of chairs one's only friends,
a lonely beer pouring out its repititious heart,
people passing slowly in red gondolas,
antiquity flowering in the backdrop?

And where is the part about the beautiful women,
the dark funeral ships on the venetian canals?
Great oars paddle the flesh in aromatic coffins,
scraping the seaweed out of our hook-nosed death.
The beauties smile with teeth like open fans,
a worldwide deceit full of earth and drowning.

we want so much love, we settle for politics.
We begin to dream of melting down the flesh,
sudden reversals: nothing happening as it will.

Escape

What if i tell you
the cobweb woven
of tedius duty
will not catch
even the dullest soul
or provide blood
for the daybreak
of the most veiled
emotion.

Hilltop house

in Georgia where a firm peace
can adequately say Now!
where God Mother Country
skim out fifty miles across the sky,
in Georgia where mud hens glitter
in the worlds of the marsh
& where ancients stand up in small towns
on silent mornings
to make history serene & more
than just the endless death of things, well

goddamn! in Georgia you can take your ass
up to Hilltop House
& get fucked in all your skin & whiskey!
greatest whorehouse in the world!
lord, it's erection, & after bliss,
resurrection & erection again. amen!
call each other up like hogs. "my woman,
she's up that hill." WELL SHIT, BOY,
LET'S GO GET HER! where women could be rivers
& men could be swimmers
they drink out of jugs & yell O SHIT!
all the way to Hilltop House.

It was beauty that killed the beast

I

The ugly women survive.
They write, they paint,
they diminish, with huge noses,
spindly legs.
They rally in wheelchairs,
they beat the odds,
and they haunt the world
with white hair.

They were born ugly,
and insufferably sensitive.
They knew they had
hair on their chin,
and they shaved.

They wrote literature
and painted
in the immaculate
emptiness
of undesired desires.
They beat their sonnets into
distorting mirrors,
and painted the dark of loneliness.
Over and over,
mothers of beauty
until, at 95
without marbles
they come to the university
like frail Martians,
human bulldozers
in huge red hats
to receive
their honorary passions,

while everyone is horrified
and depressed
and there is so much love for them!

II

And the beautiful women
write and paint and their bodies
become legendary objects
in bedrooms of dreams,
objects in creme high-heels
for their color-glazed toes
streaming up to stem-like thighs
running into red dazzling floral flesh.

They were born for Hollywood
these artists
these women turning heads
and breaking hearts,
and they know they are Venus
and sensual witches
with sculptured hair
and they carefully shave their golden legs.

So they write and paint
while they're not being carved
and smothered by a thousand men.
They beat their sonnets into agony
trying to paint over the canvas
of their haunting hips
exhausting lust and their heart
until, at 40
without clothing
they come to the ovens and the pills
feeling like Martians,
like bulldozers
puffing with balloon-empty lives
to receive their dishonored escape,

while everyone is horrified
and depressed
and there is so much love for them!

For the Mediterranean

And here is the winter season, the brute
bounding, jawboned to the bundled nameless hearts
ghosting the streets, from place to place, by icy foot
made blue to flame, crying flesh; a cruel frozen art
turning grey queens and boys to glanded ice, to then take root.

None of this snow and winter's tear for me;
I want bright harbor; this outcast season has no good light,
only thin gloom, rays cut out like cake-pieces, served plain with tea
in those awful showers of the afternoon, as snow, so slight,
shrouds the season: And all these years gone by so swiftly!

I don't want this winter of time at my shoulder
rushing each year to witness greater weakness and the greater ache;
I give you all my footprints in the snow as I grow colder
to exchange them for my simple changeless sake
now grown fierce; to live in warmth, imperceptibly, as I grow cold and older.

An ageless situation

in the bank yesterday, a local slum bank,
a ghetto bank
where they train the new bank tellers,
where they bubble over with mistakes
& every dollar is like a guinea pig;
it might not be there tomorrow!

in the bank there was a woman, a marvel
over 50 & like marlene dietrich
she could have been 100! ageless!

she had long great legs
that were sent up on creme-white
$100 summer spikes.
& the teller was snapping out 50's
& 20's to her endlessly. he didn't stop!

i just stared at her great legs,
her carribean-beach tan,
the royal blue skirt against her butt,
& i was stunned
i could feel so haunted
in my groin
about a woman who's probably living
on bank millions & an old age pension.

i walked out with $15 in my hands. shit.
it was 100 degrees, & the woman
went off in a mercedes
driven by a man half her age.
they were smiling & laughing.

in the hazy humid street
a laborer was laying down cement,
30 or 40 pounds every shovel,
& wiping the sweat off himself
& smiling, stupidly looking up into the sun.
he was probably thinking of his $7.50 an hour.

the mercedes left all the street noise to me
as it slid off like a racing snake.
i stood there, counting in the sun.

A perfect American life

a perfect american life
includes a power boat,
a cabinet full of valium, toothpaste,
& a job in television.
success includes
several weeks of "drying out"
each year
without screwing-up the resume,
& crazy foods during long
american express days which become
hundreds of mastercharged nights
with blond anemones
from the gigantic typing-pools
of divorce.

a perfect american life
includes europe several times,
& once to india & peru,
backgammon, a tennis-elbow,
4 cars at once, writing a book,
a change of career or two,
a predictable sadness every decade
& plenty of bausch & lomb sunglasses!

the final perfection seems to come at 50
when we begin to jog in earnest
& pursue a thin diet like a religion,
we return to looking 30, with ginseng,
but now with florid bottomless doubts
about the destiny of our species
& the future of our 2.3 strange offspring.

city morning sonnet

There's a lot of us who don't work jobs,
and so the monday morning hangover
is just a matter of more serious drinking
and vomiting, with morning television as a horrible chorus,
and then some beer that finally sticks to the stomach,
and later, if the dollars are there, a pint of vodka
mixed with anything: pepsi, grape juice, even tap water.

Those of us who don't work these monday mornings
don't know why the people with suits and cars
cry so much about monday all day sunday.
Shit, monday must be great if you're sober
and have a paying job and carry a briefcase.
Those of us who do nature's work: the jobless, the aimless;
it is painful enough to manage two beers and wait for the vomit.

From the expressway the meadows and the farms

Morning after morning
a rising congress of men
head toward the sun,
their feet leaving the fields,
passages of long-suffering athletes
swimming toward the cities
with huge refrigerators blazing in the muddy trailers.

A mindless child forgets to enter the barn,
he fights with the livestock
near the grass.
His fingertips turn into saplings.
It is the quiet humility
fading in his mouth
feeding the chickens that gives him peace.

At night the moon settles into the manure.
Rising from the crops and graves
the flesh turns in toward the blankets.
The deep sleep produces a ripe dream
where water begins to rock the barn
and oars begin to plow under the mysterious earth.

An idiot sets fire to the city

The tiny child began to cry
and the horses moved against the barn.
Soft death-bells were set in motion
and everywhere Sleep turned uncomfortably.
The all-night darkness turned red
and laughter everywhere came to a sudden halt.

Murder passed in the streets, gaping,
and the jailhouses rattled with shadows of panic.
The waitress stopped smoking in the cafe
and on a distant hill, under the violent clouds,
a new alien world walked down toward the city.

Reminder

So difficult to write about the adobes
where red peppers hang from dark ceilings to dry
when all you see are dead bowling alleys
filled with work-torn men, shoe-wearing sausages.

So difficult to speak of the tall beautiful women
who come to mind, in flashes, hair undone on their shawls,
when all you see are prostitutes, and grey old fists
clutching half-empty bottles of cheap wine.

One must rely on memory to see remarkable moonlight,
and one must return, backward in years, to embrace the sun
and the sudden light of loving thighs
mingled in a blue bell-shaped dress.

The lady who got famous through her dairy

and then she took out
one of her silky breasts
and offered it to henry miller,
and then to crazy gonzalo,
and then her demon, ken patchen,
and her brother
and larry durrell,
and for years and years
harvests of starving artists
clambered to her bosom
and sucked and drained
all her milky dollars
and milky rooms and chairs
and milky bottles of wine,
and all the time
she smiled sweetly
and wrote like a saint in her diary,
looking down at her great breasts
drooping heavy with so much nurture
to all the men,
the artists on their knees,
mouths wide-open,
mouths upraised
and ready for the suck;
men in diapers and typewriters.

Chicken

my taste for
crispy spicy chicken
has bounced me around town
lately.

especially to one
take-out
where the waitress
is full of magic, hot sauce

& great love handles.
her body
is a moving darkness
that fires like a rimshot when i walk in.

i think we're in love —
staring at each other, smiling in overbites
through the 4 inch thick plexiglass
zoo-&-riot architecture.

i'm the only white guy
i've ever seen in the place.
most of the time i'm tired
& hungry when i swing through the door.

& she's always ready.
something tells me that if
there weren't so much plexiglass
& race & social grace

that we'd be married by now,
& kissing a lot & laughing in bed.
as it works, the best we can do —
well, she slips me extra jalapeno peppers

& free glasses that don't come with my order,
& i stare at her, & tilt my hat & wink
& i really give her everything, including $7.28.

i suppose she does this with other guys, too.

Shoes

There are shoes at the bottom of the ocean,
fallen for years from the surface,
each mile requiring months of dark sliding
Through streams of silent creatures.

The person that left these shoes. . .
some ship has capsized, some world emptied
into the sub-zero night, someone screaming lost his shoes,
thought of his wife's eyes and fell into the stars.

Now the shoes travel in weightless forests.
At the bottom of the ocean there are shoes
Lost in wandering, shoes that walk the ocean floor,
asking directions, never listening, shoes without feet.

To ground level

to begin
with wonder

pulling words
out of the moon
every hour

to begin with a hand
resting
on a few simple facts

a recollection
of good ordinary people

a carpenter
reaching his hand
out of the heavens
with a hammer

a fisherman
handing out laughter
and desolation
on a platter
of lobster

Midwest winter

I will go out into the snow
like everyone else
in february.
That's all there is.
Keep faith in spring
like the horse,
clopping with blinders,
walking back to the feedbag.

Fun couple

With the strings of some garbled symphony
in the background, i read the Sunday newspaper,
reviewing page after page of advertisement and gossip.
I begin to feel like a monkey, engrossed with my fleas.

I live in the sort of city that people seek to leave;
one season in hell after another, where the only celebrities
are disc-jockeys and factory managers.
Genius quickly becomes a butcher-scrap in our streets,

blasted, aborted by unrealized dreams, and alcohol.
Half the population is on welfare, and the other half
are clowns in store-keeper suits: walking workaholics.
All the children look 40 years old, and soot-faced and sober,

nodding their heads continually to the beat of some machine.
There are no beautiful women here; they are all tinted sausages
turned out of predictable suburban beauty-factories.
This is a city full of knicknacks and meaningless puzzles.

And so when the newspaper spots a "fun couple" and dangles them
laughing their way through life, you can be sure
they'll be photographed against a brick wall, diffusely,
and that "fun" will mean Career and Political Parties

where all manner of ass will be kissed and kicked with a smile
and a gurgle, posing in summer whites, hands gripping gin glasses.
A third of the world starves, while the smiling "fun couple" wiggle and
wave their cold fingers of lilies into our near-dead brains.

In a city like this, the "fun couples" are just more, more
of our painted indecent desperation. In such a grey sort of town,
they join the ranks of our high-priced whores, our madmen,
and those who sit up front in first rows of topless dancing shows.

I turn the newspaper page like a sandcrab, on to the obituaries,
and to the movie guide. The "fun couple" disappears. I stand up.
I try to avoid stepping on the cat's tail. I think of myself: all things
grow, live awhile, and then we die. And some of us are photographed.

Craft poem

Sounds like a short circuit in the poet:
he yaks like a stand-up comic,
reads a collection of discarded first lines,
lights a cigar, begins eating bread-and-butter pickles,
a six-pack of beer, a bottle of wine,
and this is just the beginning:
lots of white teeth, blue riddles.

He has 23 minutes left to read away.

For a time he pulls out his dicer/slicer
stacatto, sotto voce
and reduces a rhyming, chiming sequoia of epic
epigrams into fluffly-soft toilet paper.

The eyes of the audience look sucked by fever.
Some of the eyes are cow-eyes
of sour milk, limpid and retreating, professorial!

The poet is now aiming for the girls.
Kisses! Kisses! Kisses!
He draws forth his mystic-champion poem
and sets-up 3 sobbing schoolgirls in the front row.

He reads a final poem, a short one, only 20 lines.

Hank Malone was born in Detroit and grew up in Seattle, Washington. He returned to Detroit to finish his formal education, and began a variety of careers; talk-show host with the American Broadcasting Company, free-lance journalist for major newspapers and magazines, community and union organizer, and administrator for a variety of mental health clinics. He is presently clinical director of a Detroit community clinic, as well as a practicing psychotherapist.

During the past fifteen years, Malone has had his poetry published regularly in magazines such as *Kayak, Quarterly Review of Literature, Epoch, Poetry Northwest, Chicago Choice*, and others. He has published three chapbooks, two books of poetry, and has twice received NEA grants, as well as other poetry prizes and honorariums. He is a part of CWIS (Creative Writers in the Schools) in Michigan, and is a faculty member of Wayne State University.

"Poetry," he says, "is the single thread of continuity persisting in a life that has been crowded with changes."